EDGE
BOOKS™

Secret America

Secret American Treasures

From Hidden Vaults to Sunken Riches

by Nel Yomtov

Consultant:
Jessica Martin, PhD
History Department
University of Colorado, Boulder

Capstone press®

Mankato, Minnesota

Edge Books are published by Capstone Press,
151 Good Counsel Drive, P.O. Box 669, Mankato, Minnesota 56002.
www.capstonepress.com

Books published by Capstone Press are manufactured with paper
containing at least 10 percent post-consumer waste.

Library of Congress Cataloging-in-Publication Data
Yomtov, Nelson.
    Secret American treasures: from hidden vaults to sunken riches / by
Nel Yomtov.
    p. cm. — (Edge books. Secret America)
    Summary: "Describes a variety of secret and mysterious treasures
in the United States" — Provided by publisher.
    Includes bibliographical references and index.
    ISBN: 978-1-4296-3358-1 (library binding)
    1. United States — History — Miscellanea — Juvenile literature.
2. Gold — Juvenile literature. 3. Treasure troves — United States —
Juvenile literature. 4. Secrecy — United States — Miscellanea — Juvenile
literature. I. Title. II. Series.
E178.3.Y54 2010
973 — dc22   2009005735

Editorial Credits
Kathryn Clay, editor; Tracy Davies, designer; Eric Gohl, media researcher

Photo Credits
AP Images, 9, 11, 14; AP Images/Barry Thumma, 10; AP Images/Charles Rex
Arbogast, cover (left), 16; Art Life Images/Walter Bibikow, cover (middle),
27 (top); The Bridgeman Art Library/Christie's Images, 18; Getty Images Inc./
Hulton Archive, 27 (bottom); Getty Images Inc./Three Lions, 20; Landov LLC/MAI/
Greg Mathieson, 13; Mary Evans Picture Library, 22, 28; National Archives and
Records Administration, 8; Shutterstock/Anton Foltin, 6; Shutterstock/Cobalt
Moon Design, (patriotic background design element); Shutterstock/digitalife,
(banners design element); Shutterstock/Janaka, (paper design element);
Shutterstock/klotz, 4, 24; Shutterstock/Natulik, cover (background), cover
(right); Shutterstock/PKruger, (cobbled road design element); Shutterstock/
Sergey Kandakov, (black paper design element); Shutterstock/Sibrikov Valery,
(old paper design element); Shutterstock/velora, (wax seal design element)

The author dedicates this book to his parents, Raye and Hyman.

Table of Contents

Treasure Hunting

When you hear the word "treasure" you might think of buried pirate loot. Maybe piles of jewels or stacks of gold come to mind. There's another kind of treasure that's valuable too. This type can be a symbol for an idea or a feeling that's important to us. A famous painting or even a well-known U.S. highway can be this kind of treasure.

Mysterious treasures of all kinds are hidden across America. If you're ready to read about the truth behind these riches, let the journey begin!

Superstition Mountain

The jagged peaks of Superstition Mountain stand 3,000 feet (914 meters) high.

Hidden within Arizona's Superstition Mountain may be a mine that supposedly holds a fortune. Called the Lost Dutchman Mine, its history is filled with violence and mysterious tales.

6

Around 1540, Apache Indians told Spanish explorers about a gold mine in Superstition Mountain. The Apaches warned the Spaniards to stay away. But the explorers didn't listen. Men who went onto the mountain disappeared. Others were found with their heads cut off. No one could explain what happened.

Dr. Abraham Thorne cured several Apaches of an eye disease in 1865. The Apache Indians rewarded him with a trip to the mine. Thorne pulled out about $6,000 in gold. When he went back with his friends to get more, the Apaches killed them all.

People still tell stories about the mountain's hidden treasures. But we may never know if the stories are true. Mining at Superstition Mountain is now against the law.

Edge Fact:
More than 60 different legends exist about the Lost Dutchman Mine.

What's in a Name?

The Lost Dutchman Mine was named after Jacob Waltz, even though he was actually German. Waltz and his friend, Jacob Wiser, searched for gold at Superstition Mountain in the 1870s. When Wiser was mysteriously murdered, many people thought Waltz killed his friend.

A Snapshot of History

"Raising the Flag on Iwo Jima" is one of the most famous photographs ever taken.

People say that a picture is worth a thousand words. If that's the case, then famous photographer Joe Rosenthal snapped something worth talking about.

During World War II (1939–1945), U.S. troops invaded the Japanese island of Iwo Jima. Americans successfully captured the island on February 23, 1945. A giant volcano called Mount Suribachi took up much of the island. When American soldiers captured the island, they raised a flag on top of the mountain. When the flag was taken as a **souvenir**, a group of soldiers raised a new flag.

Photographer Joe Rosenthal saw the second flag being raised. He watched soldiers attach the new flag to a pipe. Rosenthal quickly set up his camera and snapped a photo. The next day, millions of Americans saw the photo in newspapers. It immediately became a treasured symbol of American courage and victory.

souvenir — an object kept as a reminder of a person, place, or event

"It's a Fake!"

After taking the famous photo, Rosenthal took a group shot of the soldiers who had raised the flag. When asked if he had posed the picture, Rosenthal said yes. But some people thought he was admitting to faking the picture of the flag raising. Rosenthal denied faking the photo until his death 51 years later.

Joe Rosenthal

Fort Knox

Thousands of gold bars are stored at the U.S. Bullion Depository at Fort Knox.

Edge Fact:

The door to the depository's vault is made with seven layers of steel.

It's the most heavily guarded place in America and possibly the most secretive. Its real name is the U.S. **Bullion Depository**, but most people just call it Fort Knox.

The U.S. government stopped using gold coins as money in 1933. Owning gold became illegal, so people traded in their gold for cash. This left the government with a lot of gold to store. In 1936, the U.S. Treasury built the Bullion Depository near the army base in Fort Knox, Kentucky. There, soldiers would be available to protect the gold from thieves.

At Fort Knox, more than 368,000 gold bars are stored inside a two-story vault. The bars are stacked in 28 separate rooms. The total worth of all the gold bars stored at Fort Knox is about $100 billion.

> **bullion depository — a place where gold bars are stored**

Moving the Gold

Before the depository was built, most of America's gold was stored in New York City and Philadelphia, Pennsylvania. Under the watchful eyes of the U.S. Army, tons of gold was moved to Fort Knox by train. It took seven months to unload all the gold.

Information about the building's construction and operation is top secret. No visitors are allowed, and every worker is sworn to secrecy.

Security at the depository is fierce. The building is surrounded by fences. It's also likely that the depository is equipped with motion detectors and video cameras. At nearby Fort Knox, more than 10,000 soldiers are available to protect the gold.

Many theories exist about this tightly guarded security system. Some people say that parts of the depository can be flooded to drown thieves. Others claim minefields surround the area and that machine guns are hidden on the roof. Apparently, all the secrecy and security has worked. No one has ever attempted a robbery.

A Rare Visit

For years, people claimed that all the depository's gold had been moved. To prove the rumor false, U.S. congressmen were allowed to view the gold in 1974. A film crew recorded the event. This was the first and only time filming has been allowed inside the vault. A compartment filled with gold bars was opened in front of the crowd. But to this day, the rumor still lives.

Steel fences and concrete barriers surround the Bullion Depository.

Edge Fact:
During World War II (1939-1945), the Declaration of Independence was stored in the depository.

Sunken Steamship Gold

Sunken treasure worth millions of dollars was found off the coast of South Carolina in 1989.

In fall of 1857, the SS *Central America* headed to the United States from Panama. This U.S. mail steamship carried about 600 passengers and crew members. Also aboard were 38,000 pieces of mail and more than 3 tons (2.7 metric tons) of gold.

On September 9, strong winds battered the *Central America*. The ship started to flood and fires broke out. A nearby ship rescued some of the passengers who fled in lifeboats. Three days later, the *Central America* sank to its watery grave. More than 400 people were still onboard. So was the gold cargo.

More than 100 years later, a team of researchers planned a mission to find the sunken treasure. In 1989, they located the treasure off the coast of South Carolina. The ship was found 8,000 feet (2,400 meters) below the ocean's surface. Using a robot, the crew recovered piles of gold coins, nuggets, and bars among the ship's wreckage.

Other Deep-Sea Treasures

Gold wasn't the only treasure researchers found on the *Central America*. Letters, clothing, and the ship's bell were also recovered. Another interesting find was a travel trunk that belonged to Ansel and Adeline Easton. In it, researchers found a pair of pistols, a vest, and a shirt with Ansel's name still on it.

A Treasured Painting

American Gothic hangs in the
Art Institute of Chicago.

A white house, a stern farmer, a sour-looking
woman, and a pitchfork. Put them together, and
you have one of America's most famous paintings.

In 1930, artist Grant Wood was driving through Eldon, Iowa. He spotted a simple white house built in a style called carpenter Gothic. This style combined the looks of European churches and basic wooden homes. The house gave Wood an idea for a painting. Wood asked his sister to pose in an old-fashioned dress. Wood based the farmer on his dentist, Byron McKeeby. He painted the pair standing in front of the house he had seen in Eldon.

Wood titled the painting *American Gothic*. He entered it in a contest and won third place. As more people saw the painting in newspapers and magazines, it took on a special meaning. People first thought Wood was making fun of small-town Americans. But opinions changed as the Great Depression (1929–1939) swept across America. The painting became a celebration of American values like honesty and simplicity.

An Angry Public

Iowan farmers were insulted by Wood's painting. They didn't want people to think they were angry and unhappy. One farm wife even threatened to bite off Wood's ear! Wood never said whether or not he was making fun of Midwesterners.

The Lost Army Payroll

Stagecoaches and wagons were often targeted by robbers and thieves.

In July 1874, Hollis Brown and Alexander Hamilton drove a wagon out of Kansas City, Missouri. The wagon carried $125,000 in gold coins to pay the troops at Fort Kearny, Nebraska. Twelve soldiers rode nearby to guard the gold.

The wagon was rolling through Nebraska when thieves appeared in the distance. Brown and Hamilton took off in the wagon. Four robbers raced after them. Hamilton shot two men, but six more bandits joined the chase.

Brown pulled the wagon into a sunken area of land. A deadly gunfight began. Hamilton was shot dead, but Brown kept blasting away. He collapsed after being shot four times. When he woke, Brown realized all the robbers and soldiers were dead. The money was nowhere to be found.

Three days later, Reverend Henry Taylor was riding near Hastings, Nebraska. Taylor found the wounded Hollis Brown. Brown stayed alive long enough to tell his story to the people in Hastings. Several townspeople went to search for the lost payroll but found nothing. To this day, the U.S. Army has never tried to find the payroll wagon.

Edge Fact:
Today the lost army payroll is worth more than $2 million.

A Possible Clue

In 1970, Dan Conway was hunting on the Nebraska prairie. He noticed an old wagon wheel poking out of the ground. Conway showed the wheel to people in Hastings, including the grandson of Henry Taylor. Taylor's grandson was convinced the wheel came from the old payroll wagon. The next day, a group went searching for the jackpot. They looked for hours but never found any gold.

The Liberty Bell

The original Liberty Bell was melted down twice before the final bell was created.

The Liberty Bell is one of America's most celebrated national treasures. The bell represents the American colonists' fight for freedom against British rule during the Revolutionary War (1775–1783). But few people know how close the bell came to being destroyed.

On September 27, 1777, British forces marched into Philadelphia. They were looking for the city's bells. The army planned to melt down the bells to make bullets and cannonballs. Imagine their surprise when they discovered that all of Philadelphia's bells had disappeared. Even the 2,000-pound (907-kilogram) Liberty Bell was missing!

Philadelphians knew that the British were coming. They had placed the Liberty Bell on a wagon and headed north. Along the way, the weight of the bell broke the wagon. But the bell survived and was later hidden in a church basement in Allentown, Pennsylvania. The bell was returned to Philadelphia nine months later.

Edge Fact:
The giant bell was first called the Liberty Bell in 1839. Until then, it had been called the State House Bell.

Third Time's a Charm

In 1751, citizens of Philadelphia ordered the Liberty Bell from England. A huge crack split the bottom when it was first rung. John Pass and John Stow melted down the bell to make a second bell. When the bell was tested in 1753, it made an awful sound. Pass and Stow melted down the second bell to make a third bell. Its famous crack formed when the bell was rung on George Washington's birthday in 1846.

Treasure at Neahkahnie Mountain

In the 1850s, American Indians told strange stories to settlers near Neahkahnie Mountain in Oregon. According to one story, a "winged canoe" sailed in the Pacific Ocean near Neahkahnie Mountain. During a storm, the ship crashed onto a beach. Members of a pirate crew carried a large chest up the mountainside. They dug a hole and placed the chest inside, along with the body of a slave. They filled the hole, scratched some symbols on a rock, and left.

About 40 years later, stones with strange markings were found on the mountain. People remembered the Indian story and began searching for buried treasure. Despite years of digging, no treasure has ever been found. But people are convinced the treasure is still buried somewhere in the mountain.

Edge Fact:

Several people have died while searching for the Neahkahnie treasure.

Body Guards

Many people believe that pirates buried slaves with their treasures to guard against thieves. When the skeleton of a slave was found near Neahkahnie Mountain, people were excited. They believed it was proof that the buried treasure existed. Researchers planned to test the skeleton, but it mysteriously disappeared before they had the chance.

Route 66

Route 66 was 2,448 miles
(3,940 kilometers) long.

For almost 50 years, millions of Americans drove on Route 66. This famous roadway was one of the original highways in the United States. Built in 1926, Route 66 stretched from Chicago, Illinois, to Los Angeles, California.

Route 66 was more than just a highway. It was a national treasure. This road became a powerful symbol to struggling farmers and businesspeople during the Great Depression (1929–1939). To them, Route 66 led to better times on the West Coast.

In its early days, Route 66 was simply a gravel road. But by 1938, the entire length of the road was paved. The road allowed farmers to move their goods quickly across the country. It also led to the growth of the trucking business. During World War II (1939–1945), the highway allowed for easy transportation of war supplies.

Edge Fact:
The movie *Cars* (2006) is based on real people and places along Route 66.

As travel on Route 66 increased, thousands of small businesses opened up along the road. These included restaurants, motels, gas stations, and roadside attractions.

All the travel sparked some unique ideas. One of the most interesting places was Frank Redford's Wigwam Village Motels in Holbrook, Arizona. Imagine a traveler's surprise when he or she saw motel rooms in the shape of tepees.

The beginning of the end for Route 66 came in 1956. The Interstate Highway Act created a system of wider roads that allowed drivers to travel at higher speeds. In 1985, Route 66 was officially removed from the U.S. highway system. All the road markers were taken away, and the highway was taken off maps. Some sections of the road became state or local roads. Others were totally abandoned. But much of the original route is still drivable if you carefully plan your trip.

Edge Fact:
Route 66 is also referred to as the Main Street of America.

Fast Food Facts

In 1940, the first McDonald's restaurant opened next to Route 66 in San Bernardino, California. The original building has been replaced by a McDonald's museum.

Keep on Digging!

From paintings to piles of gold, America is full of secret treasures. Look around in your neighborhood, and you'll find more treasured places. Finding these treasures and the stories behind them might take some detective work. Start by searching the Internet or by checking out your local library. What secrets will you dig up? Countless hidden treasures are just waiting to be discovered.

Glossary

bullion depository (BUL-yuhn di-POZ-ih-tor-ee) — a place where gold is stored

colonist (KAH-luh-nist) — someone who lives in a newly settled area

Gothic (GOTH-ik) — in the style of art or architecture used in western Europe between the 1100s and 1500s

rumor (ROO-mur) — something said by many people although it may not be true

souvenir (soo-vuh-NEER) — an object kept as a reminder of a person, place, or event

superstition (soo-pur-STIH-shuhn) — a belief that an action can affect the outcome of a future event

vault (VAWLT) — a room or compartment for keeping money and other valuables safe

Read More

Farndon, John. *Do Not Open*. New York: DK, 2007.

O'Donnell, Liam. *Pirate Treasure: Stolen Riches*. The Real World of Pirates. Mankato, Minn.: Capstone Press, 2007.

Price, Sean. *Route 66: America's Road*. American History through Primary Sources. Chicago: Raintree, 2008.

Internet Sites

FactHound offers a safe, fun way to find Internet sites related to this book. All of the sites on FactHound have been researched by our staff.

Here's all you do:

Visit *www.facthound.com*

FactHound will fetch the best sites for you!

Index